Discovering the Jabez in You

Extend Your Borders

Jabez

Denrick O. Rose

Order this book online at www.trafford.com
or email orders@trafford.com

Most Trafford titles are also available at major online book retailers.

Scripture quotations are from:
King James Version ©1995-2009 the Zondervan Corporation: Bible Gateway. All Rights
Reserved.

Chief editing officers: Dr. Maria Peart and Sandra Martins
Biography done by: Pastor Howard Green

Printed in Victoria, BC, Canada.

ISBN: 978-1-4269-0886-6 (sc)
ISBN: 978-1-4269-2490-3 (dj)

*Our mission is to efficiently provide the world's finest, most comprehensive
book publishing service, enabling every author to experience success.
To find out how to publish your book, your way, and have it available
worldwide, visit us online at www.trafford.com*

Trafford rev. 7/1/2010

 www.trafford.com

North America & international
toll-free: 1 888 232 4444 (USA & Canada)
phone: 250 383 6864 ♦ fax: 812 355 4082

Discovering the Jabez in You

*"And Jabez was more
Honorable than his brethren:
And his mother called his
Name Jabez, saying, because
I bare him with sorrow."*

Contents

Pray it,
Leave it,
Believe it,
And you shall receive it.

The Prayer of Jabez

1 Chronicles 4: 9, 10

And Jabez was more
Honorable than his brethren:
And his mother called his
Name Jabez, saying, because
I bare him with sorrow.

And Jabez called on the
God of Israel, saying. oh
That you wouldest bless me
Indeed, and enlarge my coast,
And that thine hand might be
With me, and that thou wouldest
keep me from evil, that it
may not grieve me! And God
granted him that which he requested.

Dedication

This book is dedicated to my wife Althea Rose,
my children: Patrice, Kordelle, Tashan,
Denique, Princess, Jada, and D.J.
My mother Vada Rose, my Sisters and Brothers,
To all my Families, Friends and Well-wishers

I hope that this book will help you to
discover the Jabez in you.
A Very Special Thanks to all, for
loving and believing in me.

We love, because God first loved us.

Introduction

THE Bible did not give us a great deal of information concerning Jabez: he just popped up out of nowhere in the book of 1 Chronicles, verses 9 and 10, of Chapter 4. Verses 9 and 10, leaving the impression that they were only inserted in the chapter because the author was moved by a source of power, whose characteristics were divine in nature and that instructed him to insert pertinent information about the prayer of Jabez when writing the genealogy of the manuscript in 1 Chronicles 4. In so doing, the prayer of Jabez became the caption of Chronicles Chapter 4.

As some of us may confess, if it were not for verses 9 and 10, we would have probably turned the page for lack of interest. Now, because of these two inserted verses, the intensity of 1 Chronicles Chapter 4 goes up a few notches, allowing multitudes of ideas to flow into the minds of Pastors, Evangelists, Teachers, Deacons, and Doctors of Theology, to name a few. Let us also not forget about the many diverse groups of writers and readers, of all creeds, who are now attuned to what could most likely happen to anyone at any given moment, if it pleases the Lord—an asking and a receiving that changes one's life forever.

To-date, extensive numbers of books, prayer literature, printed t-shirts, tapes, posters, and bookmarks have been written and recorded on the subject of the prayer of Jabez.

However, you will find that this book: *Discovering the Jabez in You* is extraordinarily unique among other available literature that has been written on the subject of Jabez, due to its astute harmony and illuminating association to the word of God. This prayer, the prayer of Jabez, sends a very powerful message to humankind about God's response to prayer. God wanted it to be so and that is why HE used Jabez as an instrument, showing to His people that, when we find ourselves in places where our hands are tied, feet are stuck, and we cannot go forward, we need only to pray like Jabez did and we will see what God will do.

My hope and desire is that this book will be of interest and use to you, so read on and be blessed.

Discovering the Jabez in You

My Preferred Bible text

Philippians 4:13

"I can do all things through
Christ which strengtheneth me".

Chapter One

❦

Discovering the Jabez in You

AND Jabez was more **honourable** than his brethren: And his mother called his name **Jabez**, saying, because I bare him with **sorrow**. And Jabez **called** on the **God of Israel**, saying: Oh that you wouldest **bless** me indeed, and **enlarge my coast**, and that **thine hand** might be with me, and that thou wouldest keep me from **evil**, that it may not **grieve** me. And God **granted** him that which he **requested**.

His mother named him Jabez, she said "because I bore him with sorrow." Jabez is translated as grief, mourning, sadness, distress, unhappiness, regret, pain, and just plain old trouble. His mother's pain and sorrow was noticeably transferred to her son Jabez (And his mother called his name **Jabez**, saying, because I bare him with **sorrow**). With a name like Jabez, this seemingly ordinary young man must have been the brunt of many cruel jokes from birth. He, however, knew his God and what He was capable of doing for him. Jabez was a well-rounded thinker, one that spoke with clarity and conclusiveness. Jabez was not a quitter or a complainer; he knew that there was something missing from his life. He asked God for a change, he got it, and his life was never the same.

On April 7th, 2005, my wife gave birth to our wonderful son DJ. I was there for the delivery. While looking on at the phenomenal miracle of childbirth, I was taken aback by the amount of pain that my wife was experiencing. She had excruciating contraction after excruciating contraction. Just from the expression on her face, I was able to tell that she was in tremendous pain. However, here is the fascinating part of it all: immediately after the baby was delivered and the doctor said, "It's a boy!" my wife's facial expression was instantly changed from a look of sadness to a look of joy. It almost seemed as if she had never been in any pain—the joy of having the baby was more overwhelming and significant. Her joy eclipsed the pain completely. Now, when I look at my son DJ, I always say that he is well worth the pain that my wife had to endure in order to deliver this bundle of joy into our lives.

John 16

21A woman when she is in travail hath sorrow, because her hour is come: but as soon as she is delivered of the child, she remembereth no more the anguish, for joy that a man is born into the world. (KJV)

It could be interpreted from Jabez's prayer that his mother had no joy when she gave birth to him. She made this obvious by demonstrating her innermost feelings, "I will call him Jabez, son of my sorrow". I cannot imagine what she was going through at the time, but I will tell you this: whatever it was, she probably thought that it was certainly out of her control and she spoke her condition into her son (Sorrow). I wonder, though, what could have caused a mother to do something like that to her own son? Was it due to an absence of love for her newborn child? Possibly not, but it could be an unequivocal reflection of her traditional belief system. Not all that we do or believe as parents may ultimately become good for our children in the long run, but all that God brings about for us is always what is best for us in our lifetime as a whole.

Leading up to how Jchabod Got His name

Eli, the high priest of Israel in the days when Samuel was just a boy, had two sons whose names were Hophni and Phinehas. They were ministers in the house of God. The bible says that they were iniquitous ministers in the house of the Lord,

1 Samuel 2:17

wherefore the sin of the young men was very great before the Lord: for men abhorred the offering of the Lord. (KJV)

These two priests used their authority to manipulate and to abuse God's people whenever they would offer up sacrifices unto the Lord. God was very angry at their behaviour. Their father Eli, the High priest, knew of their conduct, but carried out no physical disciplinary actions towards his two sons. His spiritual supervision had no positive effect on them.

Exodus 20:12 states:

Honour thy father and thy mother: that thy days may be long upon the land which the Lord thy God giveth thee. (KJ V)

God was not going to let their sins go unpunished, so He did something about it. God pronounced doom up on the house of Eli.

1 Samuel 2:31,

Behold, the days come. That I will cut off thine arm, and the arm of thy father's house, that there shall not be an old man in thine house.

(v 34), And thou shalt be a sign unto thee, that shall come upon thy two sons, on Hophni and Phinehas; in one day they shall die in the flower of their age. (v35), and I will raise me up a faithful priest, that shall do according to

that which is in mine heart and in my mind: and I will build him a sure house; and he shall walk before mine anointed for ever (speaking of Samuel).

(v36) and it shall come to pass, that everyone that is left in thine house shall come and crouch to him for a piece of silver and a morsel of bread, and shall say, put me, I pray thee, into one of the priests offices, that I may eat a piece of bread.

Israel smitten before the Philistines

The Philistines defeated Israel, because the priesthood of Israel had become corrupt.

1 Samuel 4:1

and the word of Samuel came to all Israel. Now Israel went out against the Philistines to battle, and pitched beside Ebenezer: and the Philistines pitched in Aphek. (V2) And the Philistines put themselves in array against Israel: and when they joined battle, Israel was smitten before the Philistines and they slew of the army in the field about four thousand men. (V10) And the Philistines fought, and Israel was smitten, and they fled every man into his tent: and there was a very great slaughter; for there fell of Israel thirty thousand footmen.

1 Samuel 4: 11

and the ark of God was taken; and the two sons of Eli, Hophni and Phinehas, were slain.

If you study verse 11 very closely, you will notice that the Ark of God was taken in battle from Israel by the Philistines. The Ark represented the strength and presence of God with

Israel's army. Israel's disobedience towards God caused them to lose the Ark to their enemy.

The trail of death

1 Samuel 4:17,

and the messenger answered and said, Israel is fled before the Philistines, and there hath been also a great slaughter among the people, and thy two sons also, Hophni and Phinehas, are dead, and the Ark of God is taken.

(V18) and it came to pass, when he made mention of the Ark of God, that he fell from off the seat backward by the side of the gate, and his neck brake, and he died: for he was an old man, and, heavy. And he had judged Israel forty years.

(V19) And his daughter-in-law, Phinehas's wife, was with child, near to be delivered: And when she heard the tidings that the Ark of God was taken, and that her father-in-law and her husband was dead, she bowed herself and travailed; for her pains came upon her.

(V20) And about the time of her death the woman that stood by her said unto her, Fear not; for thou hast borne a son. But she answered not, neither did she regard it.

(V21) And she named the child *Ichabod*, saying, "The glory is departed from Israel: because the Ark of God was taken, and because of her father-in-law and her husband.

(V22) And she said, "the glory is departed from Israel: for the Ark of God is taken".

The name "Ichabod" means: "no glory". God's beauty, His manifested presence, and His help in the time of trouble, had departed. Is it any wonder Israel lost the battle?

Can you imagine a life without God's help? It is most certainly a life of emptiness, despondency and despair.

As we look at the wife of Phinehas, we see a hopeful mother, almost ready to give birth. She then hears of the death of her father-in-law and of the death of her husband. If that was not enough bad news for a pregnant woman to receive all at one time, she is also confronted with news that the Ark (she clearly understood what it represented to Israel) was taken in battle by the Philistines. Was that not something to die from during childbirth? She thought so. Back in those days, it was well looked upon for a woman to give birth to a son, but when she was told that the baby was a boy, she cared not for such things. On the contrary, she was only concerned about the name that she would give to her son; a name that would illustrate the anguish that she was experiencing. She called him Ichabod, saying, "the glory is departed from Israel; because, the Ark of God was taken".

For one to understand what Phinehas's wife was going through, one truly would have to put themselves in her position, so that they could fathom her spiritual, emotional and psychological state of mind. Imagine living in the house of a well-known and respected High priest. You are married to one of his sons, a priest who happens to be affluent and who is in need of nothing. You are probably the envy of most women in your community and your life is going very well. Your husband has much power and authority and he is not afraid to exercise these. He is also somewhat inconsiderate to others, but you don't pay much attention to that, because you think that God is with him and nothing could every possibly go wrong. You are almost 9 months pregnant and in great anticipation of your new baby. You feel confident that your God is with you and nothing could possibly go wrong.

Suddenly, though, the bad news begins to pour in, one bad message after the other, as Job experienced. You get the news that your father-in-law, brother-in-law and husband are all dead. Grief-stricken and emotionally desolate, you considered to yourself that nothing else could possibly go wrong, but the bad news keeps pouring in—the Ark (God's presence) was now in the hands of the enemy. Now what do you do? In her mind, Phinehas's wife probably thought that this was undeniably the end; there was no fight left, nothing else to live for and death readily presented itself as her way of escape. I literally mean that, because, upon receiving this news, she died. I could just imagine, as life began to dissipate from her body and she became very cold and heavy, how her voice must have been very low and whispery, very difficult for anyone to hear. In the midst of all this, she said, "Call him Ichabod (referring to her newborn child). "The glory has departed from Israel; because the Ark of God has been taken."

When I think of Jabez, I most certainly can see the similarities in these two instances of birth. His mother called his Name **Jabez**, saying, "Because I bare him with **sorrow**." What kind of sorrow? Why did Jabez have to carry that kind of burden throughout his entire life? Was it the will of God for him? Jabez did not think so: he knew that it did not have to be that way. He had enough, so he prayed the prayer that would transform his life forever. "Oh that you wouldest **bless** me indeed, and **enlarge my coast**, and that **thine hand** might be with me, and that thou wouldest keep me from **evil**, that it may not **grieve** me"! And God **granted** him that which he **requested**. Why would He not? I don't, at any time, believe that anyone should be living their lives with a curse; rather, to every extent, people's lives should be infiltrated with the manifested signs of God's pronounced blessings throughout. Jabez would have had the same opinion and so should everyone who is a child of God.

Discovering the Jabez in You

At this juncture, I'm more than convinced that there are people out there who are in need of change in their lives. Let us pray, while I am so much empowered to do so, and because I can feel the move of the Spirit.

Prayer

Father, because some of us are, as it were, circumstantially given birth into a life of despair and misfortune, for reasons unknown to us, we feel obligated at this time to ask you for a change, one that will balance our lives and give us peace of mind and comfort. We ask that you hold us up in the hollow palm of your hand and nurture us. Father, as Jabez prayed, we also pray, being fully aware of a definite and miserable outcome in our lives if you do not help us. God, we are asking you to grant us your favours, if it pleases you to do so; favour to be successful, favour to manage our success in a Godly manner, and favour to leave a legacy for our children, whereby they can follow our footsteps in your blessings, through Jesus our Lord.

Chapter Two

∞

Discovering the Jabez in You
God Changes Situations

Rachel and Benjamin

RACHEL, the second and most favoured wife of Jacob, was the mother of Joseph and Benjamin. She was also the youngest daughter of his uncle, Laban.

Rachel died in agony while giving birth to her youngest son Benjamin. Benjamin, whose name means son of my right hand, was first named Benoni—meaning 'son of my sorrow'. Jacob, the boy's father, did not like the name Benoni, so he changed it to Benjamin—meaning 'son of my strength'. Jacob thought that it would be better to call the boy by a name that would be appropriate for him, a name that would not carry any negative undertone. Jacob took the naming of his son very seriously, as his actions proved. Rachel, Jacob's favourite wife, who died in childbirth, did not have her last request granted by Jacob, for the boy to be called Benoni. I don't blame Jacob one bit. Would you? Let's face it. For starters, the Hebrew language is very conclusive, exact and to the point. One would definitely know why the boy was called by a particular name. People would also somehow find ways to use the boy's name against him. Remember Jacob's son Joseph, who was sold into slavery by his brothers (Joseph whose name means—'God will increase')? God increased him, by liberating him from imprisonment as a slave and placing him into the palace of Potiphar as a ruler over many. Names matter. You are what you are called by. Benjamin, in the fullness of time, became a very powerful man in the lineage that God had promised to his father Jacob.

Son of my right hand

The right hand represents power, authority and blessings. To be called son of my right hand is a very high honour. Jesus, as God's only begotten Son, now sits at the right hand of His Father. After Joseph was sold into slavery, Benjamin stayed very close to his father's right hand, which made him a blessing to his father. That is what our sons should be to us—sons of our right hand. Our sons need Christ-like fathers who will be good mentors to them; mentors that can think ahead of them and direct them to the way that leads to a praiseworthy lifestyle.

Even God keeps His Son at His right hand

Hebrews 1v 4:

Being made so much better than the angels, as he hath by inheritance obtained a more excellent name than they. (V5) For unto which of the angels said he at any

time, thou art my son, this day have I begotten thee? And again, I will be to him a father, and he shall be to me a son? (V6) And again, when he bringeth in the first begotten into the world, he saith, and let all the angels of God worship him. (V7) And of the angels he saith, who maketh his angels spirits, and his ministers a flame of fire. (V8) But unto the son he saith, thy throne, O God, is for ever and ever: a scepter of righteousness is the scepter of thy kingdom. (13) But to which of the angels said he at any time, sit on my right hand, until I make thine enemies thy footstool? (KJV)

Prayer

Father, we thank thee this day for all that you have to tell us and all that you have to give to us, your children. We come to you with open hearts and minds, steadfast to your open and intensifying glory. Let us in, God, into your infinite abundance of blessings, at this time. If we did not ask before, we sincerely ask of thee now, let your blessings rain down upon us. Supply us with open windows and doors swung wide open and when we do enter in, keep us, Lord, and we shall be kept. Lord, our children and their children are blessed also. We love you, Lord, through Jesus Christ your son.

Jacob

God blessed Jacob exceedingly. God told him that he would be blessed. It is one thing to think that you will be blessed without being certain of it, but when God tells you that you will be blessed, you know for certain that you will be blessed. God always wants to bless His Children, particularly the ones who obey His commandments. (If your ways please Him, He will reward you with your heart's desire).

Genesis 28

14: and thy seed shall be as the dust of the earth, and thou shalt spread abroad to the west, and to the east, and to the north, and to the south, and in thy seed shall all the families of the earth be blessed.

"I will not let you go until you bless me"
(God Changes Jacob's Name
from Jacob to Israel)

I just love what God does. He sometimes comes down to our level, just so that He can spend time with us, and that's just what He did with Jacob.

Jacob had met earlier with the Angels of God; he had a lot on his mind. God also told him that He would never leave him and that He would bless him. God was ever present with Jacob. He never failed to stick to His promises; He always fulfilled them. One night, Jacob arose with his family and women servants and instructed them to go over the ford, Jabbok, with all that they had. At this point, Jacob was left alone and there he struggled with a man until daybreak. (The man who Jacob struggled with was probably one of the Angels he had met earlier). Angels of God represent the presence of God; it is as if God Himself was present. That's just what it is, and He is there, always. For about six to seven hours, Jacob fought with this man.

Now, that is what I call persistence with a mix of faith. After struggling with Jacob for hours, the man may have had enough and had seen all that he needed to see in Jacob. He told Jacob, "Let me go". Jacob refused and said,

"I will not let you go until you bless me". Have you ever been in a situation where you say to God, "God, I will not stop praying about this situation until you do something about it?" You will never know just what He will do for you, until you try it. The man asked Jacob what his name was, and Jacob told him. He then told Jacob that he would no longer be called Jacob, but Israel, and he blessed him at that moment. God is willing to give us what we need, but sometimes we may have to fight for days, sometimes months or even years, to get it. However, you can know for certain that at the end of the fight, you will be coming out with your blessings dangling in your hand. Oh, what a feeling, I feel blessed already. I hope you do too. Let us pray.

Prayer

O holy one, God the Father, in you we put our
trust. Father, we thank you for understanding our
circumstances, even though they vary. We, at times, try
to make things better by ourselves, but, as always, we
fail miserably. Father, we tend to be very impatient in
wanting things done now and no later than this minute.
We fail to remember that time and seasons are in your
hands. Lord, we oftentimes forget that you made a
promise to bless us, and we know that you would never
go back on your word. Teach us how to fight like
Jacob and never to give up. When life's battle seems
hard, remind us, Lord, to stay grounded in your trust.
Please God, forgive us for our sins and send to us your
blessings. Let your love reign in our souls. We depend
on no other name but your name. We ask all this in
the mighty name of your wonderful son, Jesus Christ.

Chapter Three

❧

Discovering the Jabez in You

Jabez

JABEZ, a descendant of Judah, is renowned in that "God granted him that which he requested" (1 Chr. 4:9, 10). Jabez was also a place occupied by several families of Scribes (1 Chr. 2:55). Scribes were a group of men who are well learned in the doctrines of the Jewish laws. They were also classified as lawyers who, from time to time, would do legal services in the Jewish court of law.

1 Chronicles 2:55,

Salma was also the ancestor of the clans in Jabez that kept the court and government records; they were the Tirathites, the Shimeathites, and the Sucathites. These clans were the descendents of Hammath the Kenite, who was also the ancestor of the Rechabites.

Jabez is very well known in our civilization today, especially in Christendom. He is considered as a very popular man, simply because he prayed a short, but powerfully fervent, and effectual prayer.

If at any time you should go to a local bookstore, just take a look around the religious book section and you will find a large selection of books that were written about Jabez. He is a very popular man. If Jabez were to be categorized in today's society, in all probability, he would be recognized as a doctor; a prayer doctor, that is.

Jabez was just a man like any one of us; he had needs, desires and wants. He was in trouble; how was he going to get help? He must have considered his present situation, as well as where he would like to be in the near future, but when he did his calculations, he couldn't see delivering that future by himself. Have you ever been in a similar fix? What if you were to pull out your bankbook and calculator to balance the books, but every time you end up being in the red? What if your income just doesn't seem to be measuring up to your expenditure and you need more money? Perhaps it is a bigger church that you need, to hold all the new members or the roof is leaking and you just can't come up with the money to fix it? You may be overspent on all of your credit cards and no one is willing to lend you any more money. Maybe you are just about to lose your house to the creditors. What do you do then? Just ask Jabez! Although he is no longer here with us now, he has left us with the legacy of prayer. Pray, because it is just at these times that God wants to step into your situation—when you are buried deep down in trouble, the quicksand type of trouble. Just when you are about to throw in the towel; God will step in. Just when it seems impossible, you will remember that God can make **all** things possible. God is the most qualified for the job. God has got your back. He can pull you out of anything that has buried you. Don't entertain any thoughts of giving up; block out suicidal thoughts and look to the future with hope. Hope that, one day, you will be free from the creditors, sickness and powerlessness.

Personally, I do think, when Jabez prayed that one particular prayer to God, he was going through something very big. He needed help, but not just any help; he needed divine help. You know, like what David prayed about in the Psalm:

Psalm 17, 1- 8

Hear, O LORD, my righteous plea; listen to my cry. Give ear to my prayer—it does not raise from deceitful lips. 2 May my vindication come from you; may your eyes see what is right. 3 Though you probe my heart and examine me at night, though you test me, you will find nothing; I have resolved that my mouth will not sin. 4 As for the deeds of men—by the word of your lips I have kept myself from the ways of the violent. 5 My steps have held to your paths; my feet have not slipped. 6 I call on you, O God, for you will answer me; give ear to me and hear my prayer. 7 Show the wonder of your great love, you who save by your right hand those who take refuge in you from their foes. 8 Keep me as the apple of your eye; hide me in the shadow of your wings.

Divine Help

What is divine help? First, we must have an understanding of what the word divine suggests. When we use the word divine, we are simply talking of one who is omnipotent, omniscient, omnipresent, lovely, spiritual, heavenly and supernatural, the list goes on. The only one who holds all of these characteristics is God or the Godhead. The Godhead consists of God the Father, His Son and the Holy Spirit. These three are one; they do not function separately or independently. When Jabez prayed, he was consulting the true and living God. Divine in character (God's divine help, is the highest stratum of help, unfailing in all its proceedings), He came through for Jabez; He will also come through for you.

Psalm 121, 1-2

I will lift up mine eyes unto the hills, from whence cometh my help. 2 My help cometh from the Lord, which made the heaven and the earth. (KJV)

Here, in the Psalm, David is saying that when he is in need of help, he will look to the hills. The hills refer to places where God resides and from there, His divine help will come. His help comes from God, the maker of heaven and earth. He mentions the maker of heaven and earth simply because he wants to show that if God is the maker of heaven and earth, then He (God) would have no problem with helping him to solve some major problems (major to us, minor to God). God is our present help in time of trouble. God is willing to help everyone. It does not matter who you are, or where you are from. He wants to help you; just ask Him. He allows the rain to fall on the just and the unjust (just meaning righteous and unjust meaning unrighteous). God has control over things whose existence we are unaware. He affirmed this to Job, in the book of Job:

Job 38, 39

Then the Lord answered Job out of the whirlwind, and said, 2 Who is this that darkeneth counsel by words without knowledge? 3 Gird up now thy loins like a man; for I will demand of thee, and answer thou me. 4 Where wast thou when I laid the foundations of the earth? Declare, if thou hast understanding. 5 Who hath laid the measures thereof, if thou knowest? Or who hath stretched the line upon it? 6 Whereupon are the foundations thereof fastened? Or who laid the corner stone thereof; 7 when the morning stars sang together, and all the sons of God shouted for joy? 8 Or who shut up the sea with doors, when it brake forth, as if it had issued out of the womb? 9 When I made the cloud the garment thereof, and thick darkness a swaddling band for it, 10 and brake up for it my decreed place, and set bars and doors, 11 and said, Hitherto shalt thou come, but no further: and here shall thy proud waves be stayed? 12

Hast thou commanded the morning since thy days; and caused the dayspring to know his place;

13 that it might take hold of the ends of the earth, that the wicked might be shaken out of it? 14 It is turned as clay to the seal; and they stand as a garment.15 And from the wicked their light is withholden, and the high arm shall be broken. 16 Hast thou entered into the springs of the sea? Or hast thou walked in the search of the depth? 17 Have the gates of death been opened unto thee? Or hast thou seen the doors of the shadow of death? 18 Hast thou perceived the breadth of the earth? Declare if thou knowest it all.19 Where is the way where light dwelleth? And as for darkness, where is the place thereof, 20 that thou shouldest take it to the bound thereof, and that thou shouldest know the paths to the house thereof? 21 Knowest thou it, because thou wast then born? or because the number of thy days is great? 22 Hast thou entered into the treasures of the snow? Or hast thou seen the treasures of the hail, 23 which I have reserved against the time of trouble, against the day of battle and war? 24 By what way is the light parted, which scattereth the east wind upon the earth? 25 Who hath divided a watercourse for the overflowing of waters, or a way for the lightning of thunder; 26 to cause it to rain on the earth, where no man is; on the wilderness, wherein there is no man; 27 to satisfy the desolate and waste ground; and to cause the bud of the tender herb to spring forth? 28 Hath the rain a father? Or who hath begotten the drops of dew? 29 Out of whose womb came the ice? And the hoary frost of heaven, who hath gendered it? 30 The waters are hid as with a stone, and the face of the deep is frozen. 31 Canst thou bind the sweet influences of Plei'ades, or loose the bands of Ori'on? 32 Canst thou bring forth Maz'zaroth in his season? Or canst thou guide Arctu'rus with his sons? 33 Knowest thou the ordinances of heaven? Canst thou set the dominion thereof in the earth? 34 Canst thou lift up thy voice to the clouds, that abundance of waters may cover thee? 35 Canst thou send lightnings, that they may go, and

say unto thee, Here we are? 36 Who hath put wisdom in the inward parts? Or who hath given understanding to the heart? 37 Who can number the clouds in wisdom? Or who can stay the bottles of heaven, 38 when the dust groweth into hardness, and the clods cleave fast together? 39 Wilt thou hunt the prey for the lion? Or fill the appetite of the young lions, 40 when they couch in their dens, and abide in the covert to lie in wait? 41 Who provideth for the raven his food? When his young ones cry unto God, they wander for lack of meat.

C, 39. 1 Knowest thou the time when the wild goats of the rock bring forth? Or canst thou mark when the hinds do calve? 2 Canst thou number the months that they fulfil? Or knowest thou the time when they bring forth? 3 They bow themselves, they bring forth their young ones, they cast out their sorrows. 4 Their young ones are in good liking, they grow up with corn; they go forth, and return not unto them. 5 Who hath sent out the wild ass free? Or who hath loosed the bands of the wild ass? 6 whose house I have made the wilderness and the barren land his dwellings. 7 He scorneth the multitude of the city, neither regardeth he the crying of the driver. 8 The range of the mountains is his pasture, and he searcheth after every green thing. 9 Will the unicorn be willing to serve thee, or abide by thy crib? 10 Canst thou bind the unicorn with his band in the furrow? Or will he harrow the valleys after thee? 11 Wilt thou trust him, because his strength is great? Or wilt thou leave thy labor to him? 12 Wilt thou believe him, that he will bring home thy seed, and gather it into thy barn? 13 Gavest thou the goodly wings unto the peacocks? or wings and feathers unto the ostrich? 14 which leaveth her eggs in the earth, and warmeth them in the dust, 15 and forgetteth that the foot may crush them, or that the wild beast may break them. 16 She is hardened against her young ones, as though they were not hers: her labor is in vain without fear; 17 because God hath deprived her of wisdom, neither hath he imparted to her understanding. 18 What time she lifteth up herself on high, she scorneth the horse and his rider. 19 Hast thou given the horse strength? Hast thou clothed his neck with thunder? 20 Canst thou make him afraid as a grasshopper? The glory of his nostrils is terrible. 21 He paweth in the valley, and rejoiceth in his strength: he goeth on to meet the armed men. 22 He mocketh at fear, and is not affrighted; neither turneth he back from the sword. 23 The quiver rattleth against him, the glittering spear and the shield. 24 He swalloweth the ground with fierceness and rage: neither believeth he that it is the sound of the trumpet. 25 He saith among the trumpets, Ha, ha! And he smelleth the battle afar off, the thunder of the captains, and the shouting. 26 Doth the hawk fly by thy wisdom, and stretch her wings toward the south? 27 Doth the eagle mount up at thy command, and make her nest on high?

28 She dwelleth and abideth on the rock, upon the crag of the rock, and the strong place. 29 From thence she seeketh the prey, and her eyes behold afar off. 30 Her young ones also suck up blood: and where the slain are, there is she. (KJV)

This is a very important saying; one must remember that it was God who helped Jabez. Even though it was Jabez who prayed this very powerful prayer, it was God who did the work. Please look closely at all of this, and please do understand that it was God who completed the full circle. Jabez could have prayed and God could have ignored his prayer. If this were the case, then we would have been reading a very different story about Jabez. Thank God, that was not the case. As always, we should remember to encourage one another, in all humility, to give to God all the praise that is due to His Holy name for answering our daily prayers.

Should We Ever Stop Praying or Lose Faith?

The answer obviously is 'No'; we should never stop praying, nor at anytime should we ever lose faith. Why? Simply because God encourages us to pray always and not to faint; to pray without stopping, to pray until the tears fall, to pray until something happens—to pray consistently. The actual words of encouragement to us are to pray without ceasing and do not stop. Every day, every night, you must feel the need to pray—that's right, pray! Men and women all over the world should always pray. Prayer knows no boundaries; it penetrates the hardest situation and jumps over the highest mountain. Did you think I was going to say wall? You can't build one high enough—your problems could be as bad as a raging storm, or as high as the tower of Babel. Don't lose hope; just pray and let God do the rest. Is there anything too hard for the Lord? Stop worrying and start praying. Speak the word, believe it, and everything will be all right. It shall come to pass in your lifetime and that's the will of God for us.

I believe that we should look back at some of the things that God has already done for us. If we do this, we would have more faith in God. He has never stopped helping us; He will always come through for us. We are over-comers through His son, Jesus Christ. He is our helper; our help comes from the Lord, the maker of heaven and earth.

I must confess that sometimes it's very hard to hold the faith, but we must. Please hold the faith, ("Faith without works is dead: Those who come to Him must first believe that He is and that He is a reward to them that diligently **seek** Him"). Faith—it's all you've got! God asks for faith as a prerequisite. God also said that if you do not have faith, it is impossible to please Him and if you come to Him, you must first believe that whatsoever you are asking of Him, He can do it. It's not in man to believe, but God can help man to believe. I have also read where one person said, ", please help my unbelief." Here is how this looks. Think about God being able to do all things. Now imagine that there is a person who is in need of help and they ask God to assist in His most powerful way, but when they ask God for help, they would also have a back up plan, just in case. Now, how do you think God feels about that? When God says, "Trust Me", He is simply saying, "I will come through for you, no matter what." Don't look to the left or to the right and just keep your eyes on Him. Jesus asked Peter "Why did you doubt?" So, back to us now; every time you find yourself doubting God, just remember what Jesus said to Peter. If you believe, your job is completed and it's now up to God to accomplish the undertaking. It shall be accomplished; it will come to pass in your lifetime. If God said it, in no uncertain terms, it shall and will be so.

Always ask God for Help and Never Shy Away from It

Help is something that you will always need. One of my very close friends would always remind me of this old saying: "No man is an Island and no man can stand alone." Very true, it means that an Island could stay very green and flourishing in the middle of nowhere all by itself, but a man is not self-sufficient. He needs the help of others in order to survive (no man stands alone). Don't be ashamed to ask for help. If you allow yourself to be embarrassed, then matters will only get worse.

I can remember on one occasion when I needed help, but I was afraid to ask for it and my fears kept me up all night.

Funny enough, when morning came and time did not favour me, I thought to myself, *it's either do or die now; you have got to make that phone call.* I gathered the strength, blocked out fear and made the call for help. I got the help I needed, but if I had not asked, I would not have received the help I needed. It took me fourteen hours of worrying about something that I should have not been worrying about in the first place, compared to five minutes of asking to get what I needed. Years later, now that I have overcome that fear, I still sometimes ask myself what was it that I was so afraid of? The answer is—disappointment. I was afraid of being disappointed, which would have led instantaneously to embarrassment if the person had said 'No' to my request for help. Here's what I learned from all of that: my request for help was made to a human and it was granted. Now, what if that same request had been made to God? Would you be afraid to **ask Him** for help? I hope not, but there are still some people out there who are afraid to ask God for help. Some have a feeling of guilt and shame. The guilt part says, *you should not be asking God for that, you don't deserve it—not after what you did yesterday, you need to go and repent, pray, and ask God for forgiveness.* (Let God decide what He will give to us, from what He will not give to us; after all—He is the one who will be doing the giving). The shame part says, *who do you think you are? Holding up your head to ask God for such a thing, you are not a member of any great organization or even someone of great significance; you will not get it.* Again, leave the decision-making part up to God—He decides the final verdict. Ask God for what you need and never be afraid or lackadaisical in your asking. Jesus told the parable:

Luke 18:1-8

And he spake a parable unto them [to this end], that men ought always to pray, and not to faint; (faint here means to lose hope) **2, Saying, There was in a city a judge, which feared not God, neither regarded man: 3 And there was a**

widow in that city; and she came unto him, saying, Avenge me of mine adversary.4 And he would not for a while: but afterward he said within himself, Though I fear not God, nor regard man; 5 Yet because this widow troubleth me, I will avenge her, lest by her continual coming she weary me. 6 And the Lord said, Hear what the unjust judge saith. 7 And shall not God avenge his own elect, which cry day and night unto him, though he bear long with them? 8 I tell you that he will avenge them speedily. Nevertheless when the Son of man cometh, shall he find faith on the earth? (KJV)

Another germane text would be:

Matthew 7:7-12

Ask, and it shall be given you; seek, and ye shall find; knock, and it shall be opened unto you: 8 For every one that asketh receiveth; and he that seeketh findeth; and to him that knocketh it shall be opened. 9 Or what man is there of you, whom if his son ask bread, will he give him a stone? 10 Or if he ask a fish, will he give him a serpent? 11 If ye then, being evil, know how to give good gifts unto your children, how much more shall your Father which is in heaven give good things to them that ask him? 12 Therefore all things whatsoever ye would that men should do to you, do ye even so to them: for this is the law and the prophets. (KJV)

This passage of scripture is a wonderful manuscript to decipher and I would be more than blessed to do so, because it is important to the subject matter.

For every one that asketh, they receiveth. God, in His infinite mercies, does understand that we all have **legitimate needs**, and whatsoever those needs are, He wants to fulfill them. That is the reason why He says, "Ask. Ask Me for what you need and it will come to you." It might be just enough to get through an upcoming presentation; it might be overcoming sicknesses, rocky relationships, shortage of food or clothing, financial issues, an addition to the family, making a critical decision, or just help for someone else. He says {Ask} it does not matter what it might be for, just ask Him. He said, "To everyone that asks of Him; do receive what they ask for", but please, let's be realistic here. This goes without saying—please do remember that God is like a parent. He monitors our requests and if He judges whether our request is of a carnal nature; He will not grant that type of request to us.

James 4:3 Ye ask, and receive not, because ye ask amiss, that ye may consume [it] upon your lusts. (KJV)

This text, to some, may seem like a contradiction, but it's not. What the text is really saying is this: don't ask of God with a lustful motive, it will only hinder your prayer. God does not accommodate sinful tendencies. He considers those kinds of request to be an invalid way of asking. Personally, I think a request of such a nature will not be granted by God, guaranteed. For example, if you are in need of a car and you ask God for one, He will acknowledge your need and grant one to you. However, after you have receive the vehicle, if you then consider that it does not carry or display as well as you neighbour's does and you feel that you should also own an automobile similar to or better than theirs, that kind of behaviour is considered an act of covetousness. May I also emphasize this point: cars are made for the purpose of transporting people and things from point A to point B, as beautiful as they may seem. (One must learn to love and accept the gifts that God has safeguarded to their trust. It is in the will of God that we should have just what we get, so take the gift and appreciate it for what it's worth.)

Seek

I can remember that, when I was a little boy, my grandmother would ask me to get her eyeglasses from the bedroom. She would ask me in this way: "Please go to my bedroom and get me my eyeglasses; please look for them carefully, and make sure that you don't come back without them, thank you." Now, here is what I perceived from what she said to me: "I know for certain that my eyeglasses are in the bedroom, I am sending you for them now, so go and get them, please."

One may wonder why she was stressing the point, for such a small matter. Well, here is the answer to that: my grandmother had enough experience to know that people don't like to look for things; they would like to see what they are looking for in just a split second of looking and that's it. Where exactly is it? Have you ever been asked that question? People just don't want to take the extra time to look for things. How many times have you misplaced the keys to the car, the remote control, or the cordless phone? After a few minutes of looking for them, do you get frustrated? Most often times, some of us do. Now how do you think God feels when He says to us, "Seek" and we just look around for a few minuets and then stop looking? Just like those car keys—if you have to get to work on time, but you cannot find your car keys, what do you do then? I could almost guarantee that you would turn the house upside down, seeking diligently to find those keys; because you don't want to get into trouble at your job. In the same way, don't get frustrated with God when He says to you, "Seek Me". He is simply saying to us, "Spend some quality time in looking and you will find what you are looking for."

Luke 15:8

Either what woman having ten pieces of silver, if she lose one piece, doth not light a candle, and sweep the house, and seek diligently till she find [it]?(KJV)

Luke 15:9

And when she hath found [it], she calleth [her] friends and [her] neighbours together, saying, Rejoice with me; for I have found the piece which I had lost. (KJV)

Chapter Four

Discovering the Jabez in You

Knock

KNOCK and it shall be opened unto you. People will only knock on doors that they think will open up to them. The bible tells us that God can open any door and He can also close any door. Day after day, we are faced with numerous obstacles in our way, but only for a moment, let's just consider those obstacles to be closed doors, in order for me to prove a point. Let me give you a scenario: for example; you responded to a job posting at your place of employment and you are hoping to be the one chosen for the particular job placement. However, after being invited for an interview, you find out that there are sixteen other potential candidates also competing for the same position. What do you do then? I would say that it is now time for you to knock. Even though you may have asked God for a lead-in before you applied for the job, you still need to stay near Him (in prayer) for further directions. You have gotten this far and now you have to knock. Please, also keep in mind that the very first day that you applied for the job was only the first stage of your journey. You made it past the first level. First levels are always the easiest part of the journey. In most cases, the first level is not even considered to be a level, but it is. Now you are faced with the second level. Every level has its various different types of obstacles that you will have to face as you go forward; however, if you want the job badly enough, you must go through all of them. So you go forward to every level, where you may find the door of opportunity being closed. You must, however, keep knocking until it opens up to you. Finally, during your progression, you will eventually find yourself knocking on your last door before the big break comes. Just like the others, this door has opened up to you and you are told that you got the job. It's all yours, time to celebrate. God has come through for you one more time. He has granted you that which you requested. When we are faced with obstacles (blockage) in our way, we need to find ways around them. Never give up. All you need to do is ask God for a word, added with patience and perseverance. Remember what my favourite bible text says:

Philippians 4:13

I can do all things through Christ which strengtheneth me.

When God says No

What if God does not open the door of your expectation? Don't feel disappointed at this—I'm very confident that He is just protecting you from some kind of unforeseen dangers waiting ahead.

I can remember once I had applied for a job and, months later, after submitting my resume, I found out that they had given the job to someone else. They did not even have the common courtesy to notify me about getting my submission, not to mention inviting me for an interview. I must come clean—I was a little bit disappointed at that. However, weeks later, I found out that if I had gotten the job, management would have required me to travel very often and I would have had to work extremely late hours when needed. I could not have committed to that, so it was a good thing for me that I did not get that job. I would have left my old job and then found myself in a job to which I could not fully commit. Currently, I am still employed at my old job and I thank God for keeping the doors closed for me on that other one. Here is what Paul said in the book of Romans. I love this one:

Romans 8:28,

and we know that all things work together for good to them that love God, to them who are the called according to [his] purpose. (KJV)

God makes use of the Knocking Method

The purpose of this passage of scripture is solely based upon salvation, but I suppose that it could also prove itself to be useful outside of its original context. I have chosen to use it outside of its intended meaning, in order to introduce a simple, but significant point. Other than that, the text should still be understood and explained in its original context.

Here goes:

Revelation 3:20

Behold, I stand at the door, and knock: if any man hear my voice, and open the door, I will come in to him, and will sup with him, and he with me. (KJV)

The point that I am trying to make is this: The Lord would never ask us to do something that He would not do Himself;

however, there are some things that He expects for us to do, that He Himself is not required to do (because He is supreme). In the above text, He is standing at the door of someone's heart **knocking**, wanting someone to let Him inside their heart. He says that if that person would hear His knock and let Him in, then He would go in. (Point made.) God uses the same knocking method that He teaches to us in the book of **Matthew 7:7-12**; the non-believer now has control over the door. He or she must decide whom they will let in through that door. God will only enter if the door is open to Him. If it is not, then He will just have to walk away. Point well taken, I hope.

Our earthly father can never be compared to our heavenly Father

God is the world-class dad. He is always seeking to do good things for us. One thing that I have found out about God is that, in all of life's experiences, you will always feel the hands of God trying to do us good. Perchance one may find themselves in poor financial standing, ill health, or even imprisoned. Whatever the situation may be, God is there to help. Even before you call, He will show up. He is never late. He is always on time. Everything that we already have and what we could ever have aspired to be is all because of the goodness of God. Good health comes from Him, promotion comes from Him—riches, long life, good relationships, and punishment for bad behaviour come from Him. God is a very kind Father. He will give you what you need. There is nothing good that you could ever ask of Him that He would not give to you. All good things that are needful to the earth and the people on it are ready to be given to us by God. I believe this with all of my heart and so I live in that belief. God wants everyone to know that He is not like earthly fathers who are sinful; though sinful they may be—they will still try to give their best. However, man's best cannot be compared to the smallest amount that God can give to His children. God is without sin and there are no limits on God. He lends without expectation. (No payback.) He gives without obligations. He offers without hesitation. One of God's principles is: Ask, and it shall be given unto you.

Matthew 7:9-11

9 Or what man is there of you, whom if his son ask bread, will he give him a stone? 10 Or if he ask a fish, will he give him a serpent? 11 If ye then, being evil, know how to give good gifts unto your children, how much more shall your Father which is in heaven give good things to them that ask him?

Show your love

I love God. I also know that a lot of other people love Him too, so because you love Him, you must give Him what is due to Him. I am talking about His praise. We praise a lot of things, such as our homes, our cars and even our children, and oftentimes we tend to forget who the real giver is. If it was not for God, we would have been empty and void, helpless with our tongues cleaving to the roofs of our mouths. Praise is a way of saying thanks to God for what He has done for us.

Have you ever held the door open for someone at the mall and they just walk right through it without saying thanks (almost as if you were their personal doorman)? How does that make you feel? It's just the same with God. Set aside some time each day for Him, just so that you can offer up His praise. David praised Him for everything; he gave Him thanks for all things. When the praise goes up, the blessings come down. They are both connected (Praise and Blessings). Praise is a way of showing your honour and good pleasure to God. When you praise others for doing well, it makes them feel very good. It is the same with God, when you praise Him, He feels very good. We have a lot for which to give Him thanks. David said that "he was young and now he is old and he has never seen the righteous forsaken or his children begging for food." Why would David say something like that? He said it because God showed up in his time of need. That's why David could also say that "he would bless the Lord at all times; His praises shall always (continuously) be in his mouth". He also said that "he would never forget the benefits of the Lord". God will always enter into your presence when your environment is saturated with His praise.

I can remember, a few years back, when my wife got into an accident with the family vehicle, and it was a total write-off. Prior to that, I had put the van in the paint shop for a makeover—which took all, if not most of our accessible savings. We had to get a rented car for the length of time that we were waiting for the legalities to process. While driving the rented car, I thought to myself *I do hope that the insurance company would give us a fair deal on our old van.* I did not want my family to be taking the bus and I did not have an adequate amount of money to spend on a new vehicle. Therefore, I was strongly depending on a positive outcome from the insurance company. It took the insurance company two weeks to come up with a decision on what they would pay us for our van. For all that time I was in limbo, thinking that it would have been better for us if we still had our van. Finally, one afternoon, I received a call from the insurance company informing us that they had come to a decision and what they considered to be a reasonable offer. The offer made was quite reasonable and we accepted it. Later on that month, I was able to go out and purchase a new vehicle using the generous offer as a grand down payment with a small monthly to follow (We won.). At first, I thought that the accident would have left my family and I stranded, but God had something else in mind. God decided that it was time for us to give up the old family vehicle and He would replace it with a new one from His personal car lot. (Praise Him.). It has been three years since we picked up our new vehicle and we have no complaints. God did the choosing for us and we are still very happy with His decision. Is that not something for which to give Him thanks? That's just one of the many reasons why I say to take some time out of your busy schedule and give Him thanks for all that He has done and for what He is about to do for you.

You know, even when you are not thinking about God, He is thinking about you. God is worthy to get all praise. He deserves it, after all that He has done for us. In this world, people do need a lot of things just so that they can survive. Some are sick and are badly in need of medication; others, perhaps, just need a small amount of money to live from day to day. We may never know just what some people are going through—you never can tell. People never tell their full story and that's why we need a God who can see through us—a God who can see our hidden folders. God doesn't only seek to know, but He also moves in to assist. God rallies around those whom He loves and I can safely say, for certain, that He loves everyone. I feel very happy just to know that I'm loved by the most important being that exist: God the ever Faithful One. I know that some people may say, "Why should I acknowledge Him for anything?" "Or why should I show Him any love or respect?" Here are just some of the reasons why I think you should show Him some love. Love Him because He is always looking out for our best interest in every situation in which we may find ourselves. He could have given us far more sorrow than we could ever tolerate; but no, He takes away our sorrow in exchange for joy and laughter. Could you imagine what life would be like if humans were not able to laugh or enjoy any manner of leisure time with family and friends? That would have been disastrous for us; therefore, He deserves to be loved by us. Because of this, we should show Him our love and appreciation by spending quality time with Him in fasting, prayers and giving thanks. The Bible says, "In all things we must give thanks". Thank Him for life, spiritual gifts, physical gifts, for the people around us and most of all, thank Him for salvation, the mother of all gifts, through Jesus Christ our Lord.

Let's Pray

Father, we thank you for being there for us in our time of need, for loving us when we feel hated by the world, for teaching us how to recognize your presence in our daily lives, and for showing us how to be obedient to your commands. I know, Father, that we stumble at times, but you always find it in your heart to grant us your forgiveness; for that we thank you. There is no other love that can compare to the love that you have for us. Thus, we need at least to try to love you back in the same way that you love us. (Try.) I know that we could never love you as much as you love us, but we know that you will accept our small portion of love as a token of our appreciation for the love that you have first demonstrated to us through your son Jesus. He is identifiably recognized as a gift of sacrifice to us from you; thank you, Father, for him. (We love you, Jesus.) It is definitely because of him why salvation has come to us. Father, we thank you for answering our countless number of prayers, for giving us jobs, families, wives, husbands and more. We thank you for all of these, simply because we need to show you our gratitude and respect for your willingness to help us, your children. God or Dad, you are truly good, not just to one person but to everyone. Look at what Jabez asked of you and look at what you did for him. Is there anything too hard for you? We earnestly desire the same type of blessings you bestowed upon Jabez, according to your will and destiny for us. You know everything, including that which has not yet happened, because you can see the future afar off. The past and present are not hidden from you; night and day are one and the same to you. Who can hide from you? Who can trick you, Lord? Now tell me who can fight you and win? No one can. You are the awesome GOD, and we love you for that.

Chapter Five

Discovering the Jabez in You

A LARGE majority of people in this world may have experienced moments in their lives when they felt like things were not going the way that they should. As a result of feeling that way, they may have sometimes displayed actions of throwing in the towel; surrendering all that they believed in, at the first sign of trouble. I do understand that everyone, from time to time, will experience some type of trouble in their lives. We are certainly not immune to it, but futuristically speaking, we are over-comers, progressively, from beginning to end, through Him who is able to keep us from falling. (While there is life, there is hope.) Our problems may sometimes differ one from another; but, in any language, trouble still means trouble. The word may be brought about differently, but when interpreted, it carries the same meaning all around. One may have just been told by their family Doctor that they are suffering from a rare acute type of cancer and that, in the long run, the cancer would prove to be fatal. It could be the children, a sibling or a very close family friend who might be in some kind of grave danger, one that would need some kind of intense intercessory prayer. You may never know. In my daily life, I'm always on the lookout for the first sign of trouble and if I do happen to see or hear of some heading my way, I ever so often try to intercept it before it gets too close. As the saying goes, "Prevention is better than cure." You may not always see or have the time to prevent a problematic situation from hitting home, but if you can see it coming before it hits home, you could get a head start by installing what I like to call a Solution - Defence - Method (SDM). It's done through organized premeditated cognitive thinking. It sees the problem before it gets materialized – the method may be useful when used to withstand and combat the many different wilds of the enemy. Solution – Defence – Methods are ways in which one may go about trying to get to the bottom of their problems, with the intent of solving them quickly. Some may choose the easy way out, by applying a band-aid solution, but that will only work for a short period of time. If a band-aid solution method is applied due to certain circumstances, then let it only be for a short time, until you manage to muster up a proper super solution that will point you to a permanent fix.

Solution - Defence - Methods are very helpful; for example, the doctor says to the patient, "Your sickness is worsening by the day and there's not much that we can do for you at this point. All we can do now is wait and see what will happen; however, I did tell you that, if I had noticed it any time sooner, I could have helped you even more, but that's in the past now." Ha, what can I say? People always get themselves prepared for things that sometimes never show up, so what about getting ready for other things that have a higher probability of showing up? We must always expect the unexpected. If we practice to have a frame of mind that will always be on the lookout for the unexpected, then we would find that when we do get an attack from the enemy, our recovery time would be much faster, with less pain and frustration involved.

Another example: one regular Monday morning, a man (Let's call him John) walked into his job of fifteen years. Not thinking that he was up for dismissal; he started on his regular morning routine. While he was about to make a follow-up phone call to one of his internal clients, he heard a page requesting his presence in the plant manager's office. As he casually walked towards his boss's office, he had no expectation in mind. As soon as he entered through the office doors, his boss invited him to have a seat. Then, with a soft tone of voice, his boss said this to him, "John, we are in the middle of a transition; the company is forecasting hard times ahead. We are faced with many difficult decisions that we must make in order to stay afloat. One is employee cutbacks. We know that you are one of the cornerstones in this company, but we must make several tough decisions for the benefit of the company. I am very sorry, John, but we have to let you go".

For John, the news was very sudden and shocking, to the point where he had to be hospitalized for a few days. He did not see it coming. What could have been going through his mind at that point, when the bad news was delivered to him? Whatever it was, he was obviously not prepared for that kind of news. John thought that job security was never something that he would ever have to worry about, and as long as his job was safe, he did not have to make any extra effort to save his money. At the time of John's job loss, he had absolutely no money in savings. What could he have done differently in order to prevent his physical and emotional reaction to the news of his job loss? During his time on the job, he could have created a nest egg for his emergency use, knowing very well that, in life, there are always irregularities and his job could have very well been taken away from him one day, suddenly, without prior notice. Don't let what happened to John happen to you!

The road of life leads in many different directions; the one you decide to take will ultimately determine your destiny.

Discovering the Jabez in me

Lord, replenish what I have lost over the years to bad decisions that I have made and refill what the devil has depleted from me. Warn me when I'm about to go off course. I would have accomplished more in life had I paid more attention to your still soft voice—when it tried to direct my footsteps in the right direction. I have now discovered the Jabez in me and I am now willing to ask you for help. Lord, save me from poverty, loneliness, self-hatred, countless improper self imposed imperfect thought patterns directed towards my own self, low self-esteem, voluntary unhealthy seclusions, and stubbornness. Set me free, Lord, so that I may fly again. Lengthen my reserves, so that I will never be in need for bread. Teach me the ways of the mind of Christ, so that I can walk in the beauty of holiness all the days of my life. Speak unto me, because I may perhaps forget that your presence is in close proximity to me. Fight for me when I enter into battles, so that I will always win. See me through sicknesses, heartaches and pain. Teach me how to express more love to others. Forgive me of my sins. I will wait until my change comes.

Discover the Jabez in You,
Are you giving up so soon?

Hebrews 10: 35-39

35 Cast not away therefore your confidence, which hath great recompense of reward. 36 For ye have need of patience, that, after ye have done the will of God, ye might receive the promise. 37 For yet a little while, and he that shall come will come, and will not tarry. 38 NOW THE JUST SHALL LIVE BY FAITH: but if any man draw back, my soul shall have no pleasure in him. 39 But we are not of them who draw back unto perdition; but of them that believe to the saving of the soul. (KJV)

Have you ever competed in a marathon race? It is a very hard thing to do. A Marathon race calls for preparation, great endurance, patience, commitment, a hunger for success and the will to cross the finish line.

Competitors of marathons, at times, will experience aches and pains; however, that is the price for competing in such an energetic, time-consuming and competitive sport. Like our Christian walk, if we want to cross the finish line, despite the aches and pains we may experience, we must forge ahead. (After a storm, there must be a calm. Weeping may endure for a night, but joy comes in the morning.) (No pain, no gain.)

It would be very nice if we could be rewarded a medal without ever having to do anything to get it, but would that medal be good for anything? My answer to that would be "No". All people must work hard for what they want. Never ask another person to get water for you to drink, when you have the power to do it for yourself. (Water is used here metaphorically.) Do whatever you can do for yourself; don't depend on others to do things for you. Take pride in doing favours for yourself. I feel very good about myself when I do things for myself. No one can do anything better for you than what you can do for yourself, especially when you demand only the best. If you are in need of something and you have the power to do it for yourself, don't delay—go for it and feel very good about doing it. By helping yourself, you have displayed actions of strong will and competency. Whenever you accomplish your own objective, you will feel better about yourself. On the other hand, whenever you rely on others to accomplish your set goals, you will not only feel disappointed sometimes, but you may also feel emotions of dissatisfaction and discontentment. If this ever happens to you, don't blame the helper; blame it on your own slothful tendencies. One must be willing to contribute to oneself if one wants to achieve greatness. Greatness requires wisdom, strength and the willingness to **do**. For anything to be counted as meaningful and valuable, it must come with some kind of a price. Sometimes this will be by blood, by sweat, or by tears; but by you and not by somebody else. (Endurance, with vision, gives birth to success.) The price you pay in order to achieve your objectives will indicate the value of what is achieved. Don't worry about falling down along the way; at times that will happen to the best of us. If, or when, it does happen, just get back up, brush off the dust and carry on with the race. You have it in you to do just that. Jabez also realized that he had it in him to do so, therefore he asked God for help: he asked and he received. God is not a racist nor does He have any favourites. Jabez was just a man like any one of us. As Jabez realized, so too must we also realize. When I say, "Discovering the Jabez in you," my goal is not to give illustrative definitions only of the name Jabez. It was also to zero in on the person who carried the name Jabez and to his total unsophisticated attitude towards God in Prayer. To "Discover the Jabez in you" means, first of all, to become aware of whatever sorrow you might be experiencing. Secondly, you must call your pain (sorrow) as it is; don't just say to yourself that you are in a bad situation, but over time you will learn to live with it. Most bad situations, if left untreated for over a long period of time, will get worse or, perhaps even terminal. Now that you have discovered the nature of your pain, do something about it, like Jabez did. Call on the God of Israel for help, and then, my friends, stand still and see the salvation of the Lord. God will respond! The end result must also be the same as it was for Jabez—if it is the will of God for your life. (I said if it is the will of God here, because I do not want to be wrong, nor do I want, in any way, to mislead anyone down the wrong path about how God will respond to a person's own personal prayer request.)

Here are just some of the people in the bible who had their prayers answered by our Dad (God): David prayed, God responded; Daniel prayed, God responded; Jacob prayed, God responded; Isaiah prayed, God responded, Abraham, Moses, Josiah, Samuel, Esther, (Ask and it shall be given).

When we have accomplished all that is required of us to accomplish, God will respond. God's intervention is the only way to break down the curse of poverty, loneliness, anger, pride, sickness and many additional unpleasant attacks of the enemy.

Do not wait until you are at the end of your strength; cry out now! It is in you to do so. Cry out! GOD-WILL- ANSWER. He said He will answer you, even before you call.

Isaiah 65:24

And it shall come to pass, that before they call, I will answer; and while they are yet speaking, I will hear. (KJV)

Proverbs 24:16 16,

For a just man falleth seven times, and riseth up again: but the wicked shall fall into mischief.

When I was in secondary school, I was chosen to compete in a track and field race. It was a very challenging thing for me to do, but I was determined to do it. I know what it feels like to have a dry throat and to gasp for air: life's most precious commodity, but I knew what I had to do, and I kept at it until it was finished.

I only made fourth in the race, but that did not bother me one bit. What mattered, most of all, was that I made it across the finish line with pride, I might add. In many competitions, fourth brings home no medal, but for me to have brought home fourth felt like I had won the entire race. (In my mind, I was standing on the top box, being honoured for first prize). You don't always have to be first at everything, but I do think that you should always finish what you have started. You must cross the finish line. Finish with pride, even if you are the last one to finish. Make your effort count and others will have the confidence to count on you also.

It must be very frustrating for one to fall seven times—yes, seven times. It is easier for one to stay down from a fall than to get back up from a fall. When two boxers are going at it, one of the greatest desires of a competing fighter would be to see his opponent go down from one of his punches. The recipient of the punch may go down, but will he stay down? That definitely depends on the power of his opponent's jab, when and how it connects. If you ever get knocked down from one of your opponent's jabs, while the referee is counting to 10, try and get back up before the count gets through to 9. Don't stay down. Let your opponents knock you out, if they can (life challenges), but if they do, do not forget to show forth the strength of endurance (staying power through Christ Jesus), the will to stay. Don't forget to let your opponent see what you are made of. You may fall flat on your face, and when you do, get back up, get up, get up, get up and get back up. **If you have a will—there is a God way, way back up on your feet**, a fresh start, and another opportunity for you (Don't mention any feeling of grief, or regrets). Learn quickly about how not to make the same mistake twice. Also, don't be too hard on yourself and forgive yourself, because God has done His part by applying His Spirit of forgiveness. Sometimes people do not forgive themselves. They allow guilt to take over. Guilt is a feeling, ("If your heart condemns you, God is greater that your heart").

Discover the Jabez in You, Help is on the way.

God will help everyone who needs His help. He is the help that we need in our daily lives. What do you do when you see someone in need? Do you just pass them by, or do you reach out to them with a compassionate helping hand? I think that many of us, without any hesitation, would do all that we could to help a needy person, simply because we already know what the Master's expectation is from us. God is the master helper; we should try our best to pattern our ways after His.

It is often said that God only helps those who help themselves, but what about if we fall powerless with our hands tied behind our backs and face down in the mire? Do you think He would still help us then? I would say that God, in every situation, is there to see us all the way through, whether or not we can help ourselves. I'm not supporting laziness, but God will and has come to our rescue, even before we can think to ask Him for help. God gives a helping hand in many different ways. You may have lost a loved one and you are going through a time of depression. In this situation, He will help in ways of comfort, through His words and otherwise. You may need His assurance in an uncertain situation, where you don't know what the outcome might be. In this, He can speak a word of trust, so that your faith in Him could be strengthened. It could be love or necessity. You name it and He will help.

My trust is in Him and in all the things that He can do. As the three Hebrew boys said, when they were cast in the fiery furnace, "if it's His will for us to die here, then so be it, but we will not bow and if it's His will to pull us out alive, then so be it." Whatever His will is for you, wait on it and do not give up on Him. He will pull you out alive. If you need His help, just ask Him for help and He will help you. That's what He does!

Chapter Six

∽

Discovering the Jabez in You
The Prayer

I Am That I AM

AND Jabez was more **honourable** than his brethren: And his mother called his name Jabez, saying, because I bare him with **sorrow**. And Jabez called on the God of Israel, saying. Oh that you wouldest **bless** me indeed, and **enlarge** my coast, and that thine hand might be with me, and that wouldest keep me from **evil**, that it may not **grieve** me! And God **granted** him that which he requested.

Whose name should we call on for help? Jabez called on the God of Israel. Who is the God of Israel? Moses knew who He was; I know who He is. I also know that I'm not the only one that knows who He is, but for the benefit of those who may not know who He is, let me try to explain:

Exodus 3:

13: And Moses said unto God, Behold, when I come unto the children of Israel, and shall say unto them, The God of your fathers hath sent me unto you; and they shall say to me, what is his name? What shall I say unto them? 14: And God said unto Moses, I AM THAT I AM: and he said, Thus shalt thou say unto the children of Israel, I AM hath sent me unto you. 15: And God said moreover unto Moses, Thus shalt thou say unto the children of Israel, the LORD God of your fathers, the God of Abraham, the God of Isaac, and the God of Jacob, hath sent me unto you: this is my name for ever, and this is my memorial unto all generations. (KJV)

I AM: this is my name forever. I AM the God. It was beneficial to the people of the past, when God told Moses what His name was. God's name was also equally beneficial to Jabez, in the days when he was alive. Now the name Jabez conveys a profound meaning, and so does the name, I AM, referring to God. God is identified by His name. I AM—meaning the all-sufficient God, complete, endless, changeless, and boundless One. He can never ever change. He remains the same yesterday, today, tomorrow and forever. His name symbolizes absolute greatness, power and dominion over all things. He holds the highest seating place in the identified and unidentified domains, with complete ownership of Authority, while still effortlessly governing the movements of His creation by His own righteous rules of judgment.

He is the God of the universe. He has chosen the nation of Israel to be His special people forever.

Deuteronomy 7:6

6 For thou art an holy people unto the LORD thy God: the LORD thy God hath chosen thee to be a special people unto himself, above all people that are upon the face of the earth. (KJV)

Israel was instructed by God to call upon His name for help. He always offers His undivided attention to those who look to Him for whatever they need. He is the one true and living God; He is our place of refuge, our present **HELP** in time of trouble. He is unequivocally the one and only true God—Call Him!

The Reason to Call

There can be times in one's life when one could end up in a place of disdain, without anyone willing to lend a helping hand. I'm talking about a hardship place—where all have turned their backs on you, with unseemly ill comments, leaving you for dead. With this in mind, who do you turn to for help?

Psalm 46: 1-7

1God is our refuge and strength, a very present help in trouble. 2Therefore will not we fear, though the earth be removed, and though the mountains be carried into the midst of the sea; 3Though the waters thereof roar and be troubled, though the mountains shake with the swelling thereof. Selah. 4There is a river, the streams whereof shall make glad the city of God, the holy place of the tabernacles of the most High. 5God is in the midst of her; she shall not be moved: God shall help her and that right early. 6The heathen raged, the kingdoms were moved: he uttered his voice, the earth melted. 7The LORD of hosts is with us; the God of Jacob is our refuge. (KJV)

Isaiah 55:6

6Seek ye the LORD while he may be found, call ye upon him while he is near: KJV

We certainly have a valid reason to call for help when situations hit home. No one calls for help without having a real reason to do so. God knows the measure of a distress call when He hears one, He will attend. There are many different types of calls, but God can decipher them all. It could be an upcoming event, a long-term matter, an accident, unpleasant news: whatever the circumstances may be, He knows, and He will send help.

Hebrews 10:37

37For yet a little while, and he that shall come will come, and will not tarry. KJV

He will not stay long to come. Why? Because He already sees the need long before it is materialized. The Lord is there. He has the power to change any situation. Sometimes, when we get into trouble, we don't look to God first; we oftentimes turn to other means for help. Can you imagine what He must be thinking, when He sees us doing that? Some people will even open up to their friends before they would open up to God. There are people who will even go to the palm readers, the soothsayers, and so on, before deciding to go to the real source (God). Ladies and gentlemen, go to God. I have a motto that I live by. It is found in the book of Daniel: **Daniel 3:17-18**

17 If it be so, our God (The God of Israel) whom we serve is able to deliver us from the burning fiery furnace, and he will deliver us out of thine hand, O king. 18But if not, be it known unto thee, O king, that we will not serve thy gods, nor worship the golden image which thou hast set up. KJV

Hold on in there, God will help! He is the reason why we call. Otherwise, we would have to just shut up, to grin and bear if He had not been there for us. However, because He is there, we have a reason to call.

Let us pray

Father, we thank you for your loving-kindness and tender mercies towards us. We thank you also for the access to your throne without limits. Give us forgiveness of sin so that we may have clearance to praise you successfully. Father, the individuals that are about to pray the prayer that Jabez prayed, or one of similar likeness; grant them their prayer request as you did with Jabez and others, in Jesus' name. Father, we give you thanks for all things. Amen.

One Worthy to Be Called Honourable

When I was a little boy, I lived in a small community that was a mixture of young, middle aged and older people. Among the elders were men and women who were considered to be silent leaders in the community. My grandmother (Mama) was one of the silent leaders. She was at the elite level of the leaders' pyramid. I could remember days when people from the community would come to our home to receive words of wisdom from my grandmother. She would listen attentively to every situation; then, after hearing what was said, she would cast her findings. Her verdicts were not always the ones expected, but they were always bang on. When it came time for a verdict to be handed down, she would say it in such a way that both parties would receive helpful tips from what she would say. She would then end the conversation with a word that would restore both person's relationships back to good health. At times, I still wonder how she was able to do that.

Mama has departed now, but her memory still lives on in my mind. She was certainly a woman of honour, double honour, for the lives that she and the other elders have demonstrated. They were the ones who showed us the way– the way to live a respectable, honest, honourable and notable lifestyle. Even though I was very young and did not face any of the problems that she had to solve in those days, now that I am grown, I have seen days when I had to apply many of her words of wisdom to my circumstances. Was my grandmother more honourable than her brethren? Many others and I would definitely say, "Yes, she was unquestionably a woman of honour, both to God and man."

The bible said that "Jabez was more honourable than all his brethren," which does suggest that he was a man that held a high status in his community and with his God. He was a man that maintained a standard of living that had significant effect on others and, in the end, his conduct helped him to gain respect with his God.

The Prayer

Jabez asked God for four things. Some people will not even ask God for one thing, even though they may be in need of twenty or so different things. In his prayer, Jabez asked God for four things and he got all four of them. Notice what he asked from God and how his requests all went well together—one would have been no good without receipt of the other.

Oh that you wouldest bless me indeed

("Oh that you wouldest bless me indeed.") Every time I read that part of the prayer, it gives me a positive emotion. It makes me feel like somehow everything is going to be just fine. The emotion can be described as a feeling of joy, pleasure and boldness, all at the same time. My feelings could also be attributed to the way in which Jabez said what he did to God, (**Oh that you would bless me indeed**). I can feel the strong sincerity in his wish. It is as if he was saying it with a longing and a desperate cry for something that would fulfill his deepest desire and if his request was granted, then that would have been sufficient enough to be his last request. (Paraphrase.) Oh God, only if you would give me a blessing in this desperate time of need, for real; above all things, this one request for certain, is what I desire the most. That's how I think it sounded to God when Jabez said in his prayer: Oh that you would bless me indeed.

Bless

When one asks God to bless them, they are simply asking God for a divine favour into a world of goods. I would like to describe blessing as a permission to pass through the entrance to where goods are (Blessing is not the goods itself. The goods come only as a result of the blessing). When God grants you access to the storehouse, you are permitted to take all that is granted to you.

And Enlarge My Coast

Now that you have asked God to bless you - (Divine favour into a world of goods) you can now list the items that you desire to be for your taking from the storehouse.

Jabez asked for his Coast to be larger than what its present borders were. Some of us are in need of that request too: an extended border; more room to move and more variety of goods added. God wants us to have extended borders; look at what He said to Israel:

Deuteronomy 28:3-14

3Blessed shalt thou be in the city, and blessed shalt thou be in the field. 4Blessed shall be the fruit of thy body, and the fruit of thy ground, and the fruit of thy cattle, the increase of thy kine, and the flocks of thy sheep. 5Blessed shall be thy basket and thy store. 6Blessed shalt thou be when thou comest in, and blessed shalt thou be when thou goest out. 7The LORD shall cause thine enemies that rise up against thee to be smitten before thy face: they shall come out against thee one way, and flee before thee seven ways. 8The LORD shall command the blessing

upon thee in thy storehouses, and in all that thou settest thine hand unto; and he shall bless thee in the land which the LORD thy God giveth thee. 9The LORD shall establish thee an holy people unto himself, as he hath sworn unto thee, if thou shalt keep the commandments of the LORD thy God, and walk in his ways. 10And all people of the earth shall see that thou art called by the name of the LORD; and they shall be afraid of thee. 11And the LORD shall make thee plenteous in goods, in the fruit of thy body, and in the fruit of thy cattle, and in the fruit of thy ground, in the land which the LORD sware unto thy fathers to give thee. 12The LORD shall open unto thee his good treasure, the heaven to give the rain unto thy land in his season, and to bless all the work of thine hand: and thou shalt lend unto many nations, and thou shalt not borrow. 13And the LORD shall make thee the head, and not the tail; and thou shalt be above only, and thou shalt not be beneath; if that thou hearken unto the commandments of the LORD thy God, which I command thee this day, to observe and to do them: 14And thou shalt not go aside from any of the words which I command thee this day, to the right hand, or to the left, to go after other gods to serve them. (KJV)

And That Thine Hand Might Be With Me

Look out for wolves: wolves get their permission to pass into a world of goods from people whose extended borders are unprotected. Before you receive the blessings, do not forget to ask God for protection. Our protection comes from the hand of God. He covers us with His hand. His hand will see us through the tough times. We are guided by the love that comes from His hand. Jabez obviously knew the value that comes from the hand of God.

His hand also endows us with good investment strategies. When we invest, we sometimes make foolish mistakes. Instead of seeing a moderate to high increase, we sometimes end up losing all that we have to wolves, due to faulty investment strategies (This is definitely not the time to make bad investments). God can do all things, but if we really look at it carefully, we will notice that all that God gives to us requires some kind of maintenance on our part. We could think about asking God for a new car, but we should also remember that to keep that new car going, we will need to know that the car will have to get an oil change every now and then.

Thou Wouldest Keep Me from Evil

"And that thine hand might be with me" and "Thou wouldest keep me from evil". Those two requests would almost seem to have the same meaning, but they both have strong significant differences. "And that thine hand might be with me", suggests a request for God's hand to always be near him. In so doing, God would provide him with a needful consistent supply of guidance and protection, so that no harm would come to him. He would also be equipped with the ability to make proper judgment in the things that he does. "Thou wouldest keep me from evil". The best way to explain this part is to talk about the consequences of sin. Evil things are deadly things. If we continue to make evil our first choice; then, in due course, we will find ourselves fully committed to doing the things that are not pleasing to God. This results in one paying the ultimate price for sin, which is death. Jesus also prayed, asking God to keep us from evil. He said "and delivers us from evil". God indicated to us that when we sin, it is not because of His doing. We sin simply because we allow ourselves to be pulled away in our mind by our own lustful desires. Sin is like a deliberately planted roadside bomb. It is buried very shallow in the soil, just enough to go unnoticed, but while we are going along our merry way, forgetting ever so soon that we are journeying through landmines, the explosion occurs with no warning, claiming many lives. When Jabez asked God to protect him from evil, he was asking God to see him from beginning to end, while he was going through the landmines. God will not put us through more than we can endure. He has prepared a way of escape for us. If you look in the book of Matthew chapter 6 v13, you will find where Jesus prayed asking God to "deliver us from evil". We are the subjects, we are the ones that Jesus prayed for and, without a shadow of doubt, God has listened to His prayer and He will deliver us from evil (the roadside bombs of life).

That It May Not Grieve Me

It is not learning that one has just come into great material wealth, nor just learning of the loss of all one's material wealth that makes one rejoice or grieve. Rather, their grief is a direct manifestation of the way in which the individual processes new information within their environment. For example, I could have been a man leading a simple life and had no major concerns in the world, but after finding out that I have just come into great wealth, all of a sudden I would now find myself experiencing strong urges to participate in multiple explicit inappropriate sexual orgies. I'm not saying that this could not have happen without being wealthy, but having lots of money opens up an even wider door for the opportunity that has just presented itself. Yielding to sin will cause grief (Don't blame the wealth, blame it on our reaction towards great worldly goods—the greater the wealth, the greater the possibility for one to become immoral). On the other hand, the lack thereof (Money) could also cause one to consider participating in things that are not honourable. The key to a successful life is to have the will of God placed on the forefront of our decision-making. I'm of the mindset that Jabez knew that having a lot of worldly goods could cause him to get swelled-headed, so he asked God to keep him from evil, so that it would not cause him any grief due to his great possessions.

And God Granted Him That Which He Requested

One of the things that I dread the most is to walk up to a crowded checkout counter with an item that I wish to pay for, and after handing the cashier my credit card for approval of my purchase, she says: "Sorry Sir, but your credit card has been **declined**. Do you have another one?" I don't know about you, but I find that to be one of the most humiliating circumstances that a person could ever experience. Currently, as an added precautionary measure, I have adjusted myself always to verify the status of my accounts before I go up to the checkout counter, just so that I would never have to be humiliated like that.

No one wants to be declined for anything that they hope to receive. There is a joke out there about a shopper who went up to the checkout counter to cash out certain items. After swiping his bank card, he held on tightly to the Interac machine, while keeping a very close eye on the display of the machine, so that if he were ever to be declined of his purchases, he would have been the first person to know about it. I'm so happy that, with God, you don't ever have to go through that. The process is this: you ask, and whatever response God gives to your request will be the one you need the most. You can rest assured that even if the answer is "No", the no from God is still a favour being granted to you by Him. Remember that God sees ahead. He knows what is about to come. Just ask, and He will grant unto you what you need.

Let Us Pray

Father God, you are the joy that makes our lives meaningful, the satisfaction to the things that we crave, the love that makes our lives significant, the patience that holds on until we turn our lives around. We are so thankful that you understand us, even more than we understand our own selves. We ask of you to grant us a measure of faith and wisdom, so that we would never fall out of our relationship with you. May your unmerited favours continue to be with us – Amen

Chapter Seven

∞

Discovering the Jabez in You

Faith

FAITH is the act of one believing wholeheartedly with confidence of the existence of God and in His ability to bring to life things that never existed before, into the human domain. Faith says that without any visible proof of matter, the believer still remains confident, believing that they already have all that they need in order to accomplish the things that seem impossible, through God, by His word. Now, because the believer believes that nothing is impossible for God to accomplish, he too now has the confidence to believe there is nothing that he (the Believer) cannot accomplish, because all that he or she does is done through Christ Jesus.

Hebrews 11

Now faith is the substance of things hoped for, the evidence of things not seen. 2For by it the elders obtained a good report. 3Through faith we understand that the worlds were

framed by the word of God, so that things which are seen were not made of things which do appear. 4By faith Abel offered unto God a more excellent sacrifice than Cain, by which he obtained witness that he was righteous, God testifying of his gifts: and by it he being dead yet speaketh. 5By faith Enoch was translated that he should not see death; and was not found, because God had translated him: for before his translation he had this testimony, that he pleased God. 6But without faith it is impossible to please him: for he that cometh to God must believe that he is, and that he is a rewarder of them that diligently seek him. 7By faith Noah, being warned of God of things not seen as yet, moved with fear, prepared an ark to the saving of his house; by the which he condemned the world, and became heir of the righteousness which is by faith. 8By faith Abraham, when he was called to go out into a place which he should after receive for an inheritance, obeyed; and he went out, not knowing whither he went. 9By faith he sojourned in the land of promise, as in a strange country, dwelling in tabernacles with Isaac and Jacob, the heirs with him of the same promise: 10For he looked for a city which hath foundations, whose builder and maker is God. 11Through faith also Sara herself received strength to conceive seed, and was delivered of a child when she was past age, because she judged him faithful who had promised. 12Therefore sprang there even of one, and him as good as dead, so many as the stars of the sky in multitude, and as the sand which is by the sea shore innumerable. 13These all died in faith, not having received the promises, but having seen them afar off, and were persuaded of them, and embraced them, and confessed that they were strangers and pilgrims on the earth. 14For they that say such things declare plainly that they seek a country. 15And truly, if they had been mindful of that country from whence they came out, they might have had opportunity to have returned. 16But now they desire a better country, that is, an heavenly: wherefore God is not ashamed to be called their God: for he hath prepared for them a city. 17By faith Abraham, when he was tried, offered up Isaac: and he that had received the promises offered up his only begotten son, 18Of whom it was said, That in Isaac shall thy seed be called: 19Accounting that God was able to raise him up, even from the dead; from whence also he received him in a figure. 20By faith Isaac blessed Jacob and Esau concerning things to come. 21By faith Jacob, when he was a dying, blessed both the sons of Joseph; and worshipped, leaning upon the top of his staff. 22By faith Joseph, when he died, made mention of the departing of the children of Israel; and gave commandment concerning his bones. 23By faith Moses, when he was born, was hid three months of his parents, because they saw he was a proper child; and they were not afraid of the king's commandment. 24By faith Moses, when he was come to years, refused to be called the son of Pharaoh's daughter; 25Choosing rather to suffer affliction with the people of God, than to enjoy the pleasures of sin for a season; 26Esteeming the reproach of Christ greater riches than the treasures in Egypt: for he had respect unto the recompence of the reward. 27By faith he forsook Egypt, not fearing the wrath of the king: for he endured, as seeing him who is invisible. 28Through faith he kept the passover, and the sprinkling of blood, lest he that destroyed the firstborn should touch them. 29By faith they passed through the Red sea as by dry land: which the Egyptians assaying to do were drowned. 30By faith the walls of Jericho fell down, after they were compassed about seven days. 31By faith the harlot Rahab perished not with them that believed not, when she had received the spies with peace. 32And what shall I more say? for the time would fail me to tell of Gedeon, and of Barak, and of Samson, and of Jephthae; of David also, and Samuel, and of the prophets: 33Who through faith subdued kingdoms, wrought righteousness, obtained promises, stopped the mouths of lions. 34Quenched the violence of fire, escaped the edge of the sword, out of weakness were made strong, waxed valiant in fight, turned to flight the armies of the aliens. 35Women received their dead raised to life again: and others were tortured, not accepting deliverance; that they might obtain a better resurrection: 36And others had trial of cruel mockings and scourgings, yea, moreover of bonds and imprisonment: 37They were stoned, they were sawn asunder, were tempted, were slain with the sword: they wandered about in sheepskins and goatskins; being destitute, afflicted, tormented; 38(Of whom the world was not worthy:) they wandered in deserts, and in mountains, and in dens and caves of the earth. 39And these all, having obtained a good report through faith, received not the promise: 40God having provided some better thing for us, that they without us should not be made perfect. (KJV)

Matthew 8:23-27

23Then he got into the boat and his disciples followed him. 24Without warning, a furious storm came up on the lake, so that the waves swept over the boat. But Jesus was sleeping. 25The disciples went and woke him, saying, "Lord, save us! We're going to drown!" 26He replied, "You of little faith, why are you so afraid?" Then he got up and rebuked the winds and the waves, and it was completely calm. 27The men were amazed and asked, "What kind of man is this? Even the winds and the waves obey him!"(KJV)

However, how much faith is required?

Luke 17: 5-6

5And the apostles said unto the Lord, Increase our faith. 6And the Lord said, If ye had faith as a grain of mustard seed, ye might say unto this sycamore tree, Be thou plucked up by the root, and be thou planted in the sea; and it should obey you.(KJV)

Jesus told His disciples that even if their faith were as small as a mustard seed, it would be sufficient faith to do great miraculous things. A mustard seed is only about 2 mm in diameter; now, could you imagine what you could do by just adding about 6 more mm (3 more mustard seeds) to the 2 mm that Jesus talked about in the book of Luke?

Do It with All Thy Might

Ecclesiastes 9:10

10Whatsoever thy hand findeth to do, do it with thy might; for there is no work, nor device, nor knowledge, nor wisdom, in the grave, whither thou goest. (KJV)

James 2:18-20

18Yea, a man may say, Thou hast faith, and I have works: shew me thy faith without thy works, and I will shew thee my faith by my works. 19Thou believest that there is one God; thou doest well: the devils also believe, and tremble. 20But wilt thou know, O vain man, that faith without works is dead?

It would be very nice if we could just hold out our hand and every time we needed something, it would just fall right into it. However, as you already know, life is not like that. We must apply to our work and God will do for us far more than we could ever imagine. Look at the Apostle Paul, and what was said by him, "Paul planted and Apollos watered, but the increase came from God". See, even God has to work. Faith and work goes hand in hand. If you put them together, they will get God's attention and then the increase will come. The increase is God's way of showing how much He loves us. In tough times like these, I know that there are people out there who could use some help, so why not ask Him for help? May God continue to bless you, in Jesus' name.

Chapter Eight

∽

Discovering the Jabez in You

We Need To Pray

WHILE writing this book, I thought that it would have been very important to include a chapter on the area of Prayer. "Why?" you may ask. Well, simply because I could not have written a book about Jabez if I did not put some quality time on the subject of prayer.

Of the many groups of people that are acquainted with the name Jabez, if you ask them who he was, they would probably use the word prayer while describing him. Therefore, it would have been somewhat of an oversight on my part if I did not include some important technicalities of prayer in this book.

Many people already have a vivid understand of what prayer is and what it can do for them. Some people will tell you that they know how and what to pray for. Many will also tell you that they were taught how to pray by loved ones from a very tender age. Don't fool yourselves, a majority of people out there do know how to pray – Christians and non-Christians alike—contrary to popular belief that they don't.

When I was just a little boy, I was taught how to pray by members of my family. Prayer was a major component in the home where I grew up. There were prayers for when I went off to sleep, for when I woke up in the mornings, for breakfast, lunch and for dinner. I can also remember praying at school in the mornings during devotion. School devotions were a must. I can also remember my parents waking us up early in the mornings, just so that we would not be late for morning devotions at school. I don't know if they still do morning devotions at my old school, but today, I can still recite a few prayers that I had to memorize from my old school days and from my Grandmother praying out aloud at nights just before she went off to sleep.

As a father, I always instruct my children towards the directives of my grandmother's teachings. I don't force them, but I teach them the importance of prayer, in hope that one day they too would do the same for their children. Prayer must be carried over from one generation to the next. It should never depart from the family. It should continue to be like smoke, ascending to the heavens.

My family started me off with small recitation prayers and then, as I grew older, they taught me how to say freely what I wanted to say to God in prayer. In the days when I just started to get the grasp on praying, my prayers were sometimes long but most of the time very short. Oftentimes, when I prayed the short prayers, I wondered if God had considered me lazy for praying such short prayers. Now that I'm older, I understand that some prayers can be short and some can be very long. As for me, I always honestly say what needs saying, regardless of how long or short my prayers may be. When you pray, never feel like you are boring God, because He always pays attention to what the least one of us has to say to Him.

What Is Prayer?

Prayer can be described as talking with God. It's not complicated. I must admit though, that while prayer itself seems very simple and not difficult to explain, we must keep in mind that there are many different echelons of prayer. Nevertheless, for now, I will keep my explanations very simple and later on, I will explain some of the many diverse groups of prayers in a more descriptive way.

God gave humans the ability to communicate with each other in a very special way. We are the only earthly life form that has the ability to exchange words between each other in the way that we do. When we speak, others can understand what we are saying. It is a natural phenomenon; a special gift from God.

During your personal prayer moments, you can decide if you would like to pray out aloud or by internal meditation. You also have the option to pray with your eyes opened or closed, the choices are always ours. Most people, when they pray, do so with their eyes closed. Ninety percent of the time when I pray, I do so with my eyes closed. I don't have any strict regulation on that, but it has become a habit for me. I think the main reason why most people pray with their eyes closed is because keeping their eyes closed during prayer moments intensifies concentration. Concentration allows prayer warriors to close out any possible hindrances around them, so that they can focus their attention on a single objective. I pray with my eyes open only when I'm driving, working, or walking and usually those prayers are generally very short ones. Prayers can also be prayed while standing up; you don't have to go down on your knees, but there are instances when the occasion may call for you to be on your knees. One very important point that I must make is this: one must remember that there is a big difference between talking to a human and talking with God. When we talk together as humans, we do so in a manner that brings about a sense of equality; however, when we communicate (Pray) with God, we should remember that He is the Master, the Sovereign one—maker and creator of all humankind. When we go to Him, there must be reverence and respect. He is not like us, He is higher than we are and when we approach Him, we should keep those thoughts in the forefront of our minds. I will try to give you the big picture about the point that I am trying to make about God, and how we should approach Him. Some humans, even though all were created equal, possess certain authority, which may allow them to be seated in high lavish respectable places that cannot be approached by anyone without having been granted permission. You dare not violate their directives or else you could be killed or placed in prison. Now God, who is above all, who sits in a place where no man can enter, but He does not require His children to have any special kind of documentation or permission to enter into His presence (by way of prayer). Nonetheless, when we approach Him, we should do so in the spirit of love, reverence, adoration and respect. Notice I did not mention fear (Being afraid) because, when we approach God's throne, we should enter there in the spirit of love. The Bible said that we should go boldly to the throne of grace. If we Love Him, then we have no need to be afraid of Him. Love eliminates fear. Fear gives birth to torment, and torment shows the way to isolation.

Hebrews 4:16

16Let us therefore come boldly unto the throne of grace, that we may obtain mercy, and find grace to help in time of need. (KJV)

There are certain places and things that we should set apart (Holy) solely for the purpose of prayer. When I was much younger in the faith, a few of my friends from our local church body came over to my house for a prayer meeting and while they were praying, God spoke a divine message through one of the Senior leaders among the group, saying that I needed to set up an altar in my home. At first, I did not understand what God meant. I thought He was asking me to get wood, stones or glass and build an altar, but about six months later, after talking with one of my friends, I found out that God was only simply telling me to consecrate unto Him a place in my home where I could spend time there with Him in prayer. Sometimes, we are not organized in prayer and God just wants us to get organized, by setting things in order. Designating a place where we could meet with Him on a regular basis in prayer is a good place to start.

When we pray, we sometimes include certain objects, such as our Bible, olive oil and possibly head covering (Head covering, for those who require it). Those objects should be clean and set apart, not mingled with any other unclean things. Why? Let's put it this way—when we pray, we methodically enter into a spiritually consecrated place where hallowed fellowship commences with a Holy God. It is a place of meeting, where true communication takes place with the Supreme Ruler.

Matthew 18:20

20 For where two or three are gathered together in my name, there am I in the midst of them. (KJV)

Lip Service

Recently, I was talking with one of my friends. During the conversation, while he was in the middle of making one of his strong points, I found myself drifting off into deep thoughts, imagining that I was laying on a beach somewhere down in the Caribbean. Have you ever attended a presentation where, while the presenter was presenting, you tried to find something to occupy your time, so that you would not get drowsy and fall asleep? I think some of us are guilty of doing something like that. What about when we are praying? Do we fall asleep on God and say stupid things that don't make sense, or do we stand at attention while praying.

Many late nights after getting home from a hard day's work, I kneel at my bedside to pray, only to find myself still kneeling there two or so hours later on wondering what had happened, and why was I still kneeling at my bedside. God knows that humans do get tired at times, but I don't think He is pleased with us when we fall asleep while talking to Him. How would you like it if, every time you talked with your friends, during the conversation they would fall asleep on you? God wants us to be on the ball when we talk to Him (Remember, it's a two-way conversation). He also wants us to focus on what we are saying to Him. We must also be very truthful about the things that we are saying to Him. Don't make promises that you cannot keep, also don't make impulsive requests that, in the long run, may ultimately work towards bringing about your final demise. How about people who praise God with their lips, while their hearts say something else? Remember, God knows everything. If you love Him, He knows and if you don't, He knows. If you need more time to get to know Him, ask Him to help you to do so, and He will show you the way. God also specializes in the basics. I can remember, when I first came to Him I was lost. I hadn't the slightest idea, but as time went on, I managed to gain knowledge from His teachings, which helped me to be where I am today. Today, I am still far off from where I should be in Him, but I am very confident that, with time, I will gain the wisdom and knowledge that I need to get me closer to where I should be in Him.

Matthew 15:8

8 This people draweth nigh unto me with their mouth, and honoureth me with their lips; but their heart is far from me. (KJV)

To God, Through Jesus Christ

When I pray, to whom do I pray? You may already know the right answer, but the answer to that question is God the Father. He is the same God to whom Jabez prayed. Jesus is the Son of God, He is also known as the Word of God. The Holy Spirit, who is also known as the Comforter, is the power of God. The three are one. Jesus is not the Father, neither is the Holy Spirit the Father, but the three exist as one entity, agreeing on everything as one. Jesus is from God the Father. He sits at the right hand of the Father. The Holy Spirit: The Comforter resides with God and does what God ask Him to do. When we pray, we should address our prayers to God the Father, through Jesus Christ the Son.

Matthew 6:9-13 (KJV)

9After this manner therefore pray ye: Our Father which art in heaven, Hallowed be thy name. 10Thy kingdom come, Thy will be done in earth, as it is in heaven. 11Give us this day our daily bread. 12And forgive us our debts, as we forgive our debtors. 13And lead us not into temptation, but deliver us from evil: For thine is the kingdom, and the power, and the glory, forever. Amen. (KJV)

Some people may say, "So then, if we address our prayers only to God then what role does Jesus play?" The answer is: Jesus plays a very active role in the way in which our prayers are presented to the Father. He makes intercession to the Father on our behalf (He is our attorney). He knows our situation very well.

Romans 8:34

34Who is he that condemneth? It is Christ that died, yea rather, that is risen again, who is even at the right hand of God, who also <u>maketh intercession for us</u>.

On the other hand, the Holy Spirit who is our Helper also does something very special for us when we pray. He, as well, intervenes in our prayers to God. The Bible said, "With groaning, which cannot be spoken". Therefore, you see the order. God has everything under control. When we pray, the situation is already taken care of, even before the prayer leaves our lips. God hears it and has a plan for it. Now that we know all this, I still don't see the real reason why some people are still not extraordinarily faithful in prayer, knowing very well that we are not alone, even though life's circumstances make us think that we are.

Prayer is not a simple thing, and it should not be taken lightly. Prayer is a very special creative communication tool that God, through His infinite wisdom, has implemented as a means of having dialog between Him and His saints. The order of prayer is a well thought out plan that is only visible and useful to those who seek to find out its mysterious values.

Romans 8:26 (KJV)

26 Likewise the Spirit also helpeth our infirmities: for we know not what we should pray for as we ought: but the Spirit itself maketh intercession for us with groaning which cannot be uttered.

Going the Extra Mile In Order To Maintain a Healthy Prayer Life

I must admit that it sometimes gets very hard to maintain a continuous prayer lifestyle. You know the many different obstacles that take away valuable time from us. When it's not the unexpected overtime at work, which you cannot refuse to do, it's the overbooked appointment schedule. Sometimes it could be just plain old laziness, five minutes on the pull-out, and before you know it; you are out for the night, sound asleep, forgetting to pray—have you every been there?

Because prayer plays such a very important role in our lives, we may have to drop some of the things that are not so important and move towards making some well needed adjustments, so that we could get our prayer life back on the right track. I would like to suggest some ideas on how we can get over some of those sluggish prayer moments.

Try always to maintain a prayerful heart. Allow yourself to have spontaneous prayer moments. Set up a prayer timetable and try to stick to it. During the course of the day, concentrate on and log the things that you need to prayer concerning. At some point, in one of your prayer session, present your list before God in its entirety. If need be, team up with a person who you know would be a good prayer partner. He or she will help you to be more accountable to your prayer obligations. Set prayer goals, and try to break your own record. Spend some valuable prayer time in seclusion, one on one with The Lord.

Matthew 14:23

²³ **And when he had sent the multitudes away, he went up into a mountain apart to pray: and when the evening was come, he was there alone. (KJV)**

Matthew 6:6

⁶**But thou, when thou prayest, enter into thy closet, and when thou hast shut thy door, pray to thy Father which is in secret; and thy Father which seeth in secret shall reward thee openly. (KJV)**

You would be very surprised to know how much you can accomplish just by praying alone, or with someone else who really has the gift of praying and who also has much to pray for. We certainly do have a lot to pray for in this day and age and we definitely cannot afford to fall back now. I certainly do not want to be held back from my blessings simply because of procrastination and poor organizational skills. As long as it's in my power to do something about it, I would certainly like to give it a try, by going the extra mile, even at the cost of being away from my family or the general populace for some short while. In the long run, I can assure you that it will benefit you in ways that you could not imagine. Don't count time spent in prayer as time wasted, but rather, count time spent in prayer as time gained. I do have somewhat of an understanding of how important it is to maintain a steady prayer life with God. If you would stop and take a look at what is taking place in the world today, you would get a glimpse of what is yet to come (We have a lot to pray for). I do not want to scare anyone or to make this chapter out to be an end time message, but the fact still remains that we need to pray. Prayer lifts our heavy burdens. Prayer helps to ease our troubled minds. When we pray about a situation, that is it, it's done – leave it there and God will take care of it. It doesn't matter what it is, He will never tell us that it's too heavy for Him. Some people pray and after praying, they get up from prayer with the same old worrisome burden on their minds. No, it's not like that. God's people should just pray and leave the worrying to God. I'm not saying that the mountains will always move right away, but I will tell you this, God will move the mountain in due season. God always has a way of working things out; He will surprise you every time.

Prayer and Fasting

Fasting can be described as a temporary withdrawal from food, drink, or any other activities that are pertaining to pleasure or of any such thing. It is a time when one would afflict their bodies, so to speak, with the intent of having their spirit gaining leadership and control over the flesh. The spirit and the flesh are at war daily, each one hoping to have dominion over the other. God is Spirit; He has no dealings with the flesh. By afflicting our flesh through the process of fasting, our sprit gains control over our defeated flesh. Now when the spirit gains dominion over the flesh, God will enter in and have His way with us. We will also have the power to fight and defeat the adversary with our weapons of war.

Fasting can be surprisingly effective when it is combined with prayer. When one goes on a fast, it is usually for a predetermined timeline, a couple of hours, a day, two days or more (Health permitting). Fasting plays a very important role in a person's life, because there are times when prayer alone just won't do. Jesus said that there are instances when you will need the combined power of both prayer and fasting, in order to break down certain stronghold of the enemy. He said, "Some of these only go out by prayer and fasting" (Glory to God).

I can remember one year, around August or so, when I was very sick with the flu for about seven or so days. Due to my illness, I did not have the desire to eat anything. I must have gone about four days without food. God had put me on an unavoidable fasting. When I was into about my fourth day without food, God showed me a dream. The dream was what I needed to see at the time. It showed me everything that I was going through and what I needed to do in order to escape the pitfalls of the enemy. If it was not for that fasting, I don't think that I would have managed to escape the wilds of the enemy (Fasting does work).

What's The Occasion?

There are many different types of prayers. I will just name a few.

Let me try to explain. In our day-to-day life, we go about communicating one to another on different topics, shifting from one event to the next, whatever is needful to discuss at that given moment: for example, a vote of thanks, showing appreciation, a request for something, offering up ourselves as proxy for another, dedication and so on. In prayer, we do the same thing. When we pray, we pray according to the occasion. Let's say, for example, that two persons are engaged in a conversation. While they are talking, they usually incorporate more than one subject within context. It doesn't make any sense to talk outside of context. Keep in mind; though, that during the conversation, there might be more than one thought being discussed within the same context. During a prayer session, you can incorporate more than one need in the same prayer. For example, you can make supplication for more strength, thanksgiving, dedication, praise, or so on, in the same prayer session. Any one of the above reasons for praying can also be prayed on an individual basis. Take, for example, in the book of 1 Chronicles, Jabez's prayer to God was a prayer of **Supplication.** Supplication means to make an appeal or plead with someone for something. I'm of the mindset that after Jabez's request was granted by God, he may have also prayed a prayer of thanksgiving to God for answering His prayer. Prayer of thanksgiving means to speak words of gratitude, appreciation and recognition to God for something that He has done for you. That's how I would like to end this book, by giving God thanks in prayer.

Prayer

Father, words cannot explain how thankful we are towards you; for what you have done for us. You have blessed us with your love, joy and peace. We cannot afford to be ungrateful towards you. Father, we thank you for giving us our daily supply of food on our table, clothes on our backs, for good health and strength. We also thank you for protecting us from the many attacks of the enemy, also for giving us the endurance to complete our God-given tasks. God, we thank you and praise you through no other name, but the name of Jesus the Christ the anointed One - Amen

And God
Granted him
That which he requested

Altar Call

No Inferiority Complex Here

It is not arrogant to believe that you are just as precious as the person sitting next to you on the bus, nor is it bad behaviour to speak boldly to the person who is asking you the questions during an interview. God wants us to be strong, bold and courageous—not fearful and weak. He told us to come boldly to His throne when we pray. We do this because we have a good relationship with Him.

God loves us and we should love Him too. When love comes in, all fears are gone. Fear sets up barriers between loved ones and we do not want any barriers to hinder our relationship with God.

We were all created equal in God's image and in His likeness. We are His children. God listens to the cries of His children, regardless of race, culture or stature. We all have the same opportunity into His abundant blessing. That is why, my friends, I would like to pray a very special prayer for all conditions that are listed below and also for other conditions that were not mentioned. Please feel free to add in any supplementary requests when you pray this prayer

People without Jobs

Cancer

Aids

Add your category of sickness

Those who have lost a loved one

Lack of food, money and clothing,

Praying for a addition to your family

Need a place to live, transportation. Add more in.

Disorderly children

Need to relocate

Need to sell your house - add your category in

Let's pray

Father, to you alone, who is able to do all things, we thank you for what you are about to do for your people. Father, we praise you and lift up your name to the highest heavens. There is none like you and no one to come that will be like you. You are the awesome wonder, never to change today or tomorrow. Father, I have written down many categories of things that I would like to pray for. I am asking you to honour them, Father, and to help all those who are suffering from any of the conditions listed above. Father, if they are sick, heal like only you can; if they are in need, then give the way only you can; if they are sad, comfort them the way only you do; and Father, for the things that we have not mentioned, please fail not to grant it unto us, in Jesus' name we pray, Amen.

Discovering the Jabez in You

My Final Words

A T times, we are faced with obstacles and disappointments in our lives and we oftentimes wonder if the problems will ever end—we never know what a new day may have in store for us. Some days are good and some days are not so good; yet, we hope for days filled with satisfaction, without restrictions or compromises. Unfortunately, sometimes that never happens, and at the end of the day, we find ourselves in troublesome predicaments that are very difficult to deal with. When one finds oneself in a hard place, which proves difficult and stressful, one should consider calling for help. Jabez did. Remember, help is just a prayer away. God specializes in the things that seem impossible. With God, all things are possible.

The Bible tells us that we must have faith. We need the power of faith to overcome our day-to-day challenges (It is through faith that we overcome the world). Faith is a prerequisite in all the things that we do and say ("And without faith, it is impossible to please God – those who come to Him, must first believe that He is and that He is a reward to them that diligently seek after Him"). Jesus said that we do not need a lot of faith, in order to command circumstances to comply with our order. Here is what Jesus said: "If you have faith as much as a mustard seed, you are able to <u>command</u> the mountain to move out of its place and it shall obey". The Bible says that, "God calls things that are not, as though they were". By His words, they come forth and are made manifest. We are all living testimonies of the miracles of God. God called us from nothing to a life of actualization. We are living examples of a manifested truth. May He continue to show to us the purpose for our existence, arming us also with the necessary tools required to accomplish our set goals and fitting us into our most desired areas in life. Go now, and engrave your mark on life.

Benediction:

May the God of our Lord and Saviour Jesus Christ: save and keep you in all your ways until He comes. Amen.

Discovering the Jabez in You

The End